The Grave of the Right Hand

The Grave of the Right Hand

By CHARLES WRIGHT

 WESLEYAN UNIVERSITY PRESS
Middletown, Connecticut

Acknowledgement is gratefully made to the following periodicals, in the pages of which some of the poems in this volume were first published: *Abraxas, Arena, Choice, The Denver Quarterly, The Far Point, The Nation, The New Orleans Review, The New Yorker, The North American Review, Northwest Review, The Oberlin Quarterly, Poetry, Poetry Northwest, The Red Cedar Review, Statements/Midwest,* and *Tennessee Poetry Journal.*

The poems "The Daughters of Blum," "Homecoming," and "Piccola Elegia" (under the title "Smoke") were first published in *The New Yorker.*

The poems "Addendum," "Eye," "The Grave of the Right Hand," "Half-Moon," "Illumination," "In the Midnight Hour," "The Killing," "The Offering," and "The Self-Portrait" were first published in *Poetry.*

The poems included in the first two parts of this volume, "The Night Watch" and "Departures," were published in Canada in 1968 by The House of Anansi Press of Toronto in a limited edition of a booklet entitled *The Dream Animal* and are copyrighted in Canada by the publisher.

LIBRARY OF CONGRESS CATALOGING IN PUBLICATION DATA

PS3573.R52G7
Wright, Charles, 1935–
  The grave of the right hand. Middletown, Conn., Wesleyan University Press
[1970]
66 p. 21 cm. (The Wesleyan poetry program)

I. Title
PS3573.R52G7   811'.5'4   76-105510MARC
ISBN 0-8195-2051-9

All inquiries and permissions requests should be addressed to the Publisher, Wesleyan University Press, 110 Mt. Vernon Street, Middletown, Connecticut 06457

Distributed by Harper & Row Publishers, Keystone Industrial Park, Scranton, Pennsylvania 18512

Manufactured in the United States of America
First printing, 1970; second printing, 1984

For Holly, SMB

CONTENTS

The Lost Displays

The Night Watch

The daughters of Blum
Are growing older.
These chill winter days,
Locking their rooms, they
Seem to pause, checking,

Perhaps, for the lights,
The window curtain,
Or something they want
To remember that
Keeps slipping their minds.

You have seen them, how
They stand there, perplexed,
— And a little shocked —
As though they had spied,
Unexpectedly,

From one corner of
One eye, the lives they
Must have left somewhere
Once on a dresser —
Gloves waiting for hands.

This one island
Has slipped
Summer's harness. Its
Towns stand
Dull in their fields
Like patient
Oxen, white-kneed
And sad, with
No one to please.
The beaches, the flat-faced
Hotels all
Are deserted, their
Shopfronts are shuttered. The
Townsfolk talk
Only in off
Tones, or not
At all. Over
Their shoulders they
Hear the drop
Of chains,
The dark winds start
Behind the Urals.

HOMECOMING

(M. W. W., 1910–1964)

I sit on my father's porch.
It is late. The evening, like
An old dog, circles the hills,
Anxious to settle. Across
Our road the fields and fruit trees,
Hedgerows and, out beyond, in
Another state, the misty
Approaches to the mountains,
Go quietly dark. In the
Close corners of the yard white
Cape jasmine blossoms begin
To radiate light, become
Cold eyes. Into the sky the
Soft, loose Milky Way returns,
Gathering stars as it swarms
Deeper into the west. Now
Fireflies, like drops of blood, squirt
Onto the stiff leaves of the
Ivy vines, onto the bell
Lilies. Now I remember
Why I am here, and the sound
Of a breathing no longer
My own cuts through as I wait
For what must happen, for the
Flurry of wings, your dark claw.

1.

Outside, in the night, a wind
Rises, clacking the dry fronds
Of the jacaranda tree.
Beside me — in that locked room
I may not hope to approach —
You sleep as the birds must sleep,
Their easy breathing. And I,
Awake now, hearing the wind,
The skeletal leaves, the come
And go of your cool breath,
Realize what has happened
And start to feel vague, as some
Wound might feel, reopened, whose
Infection has just returned.

2.

Hung in the gathering leaves
(Like cages, I say), the late
Oranges swing in the rain,
Balancing, now, back and forth.
We watch them through the window.
If cages, you answer, they
Must be for crickets, bringers
Of good luck, they are so small.
True . . .

        However, that black spot
On each — that seems to lean out,
That seems to proffer itself —
Is not from any cricket,
No, but something else which has
No name, and will not ever sing.

TO A FRIEND WHO WISHED ALWAYS TO BE ALONE
  (William Martin, dead in Georgia)

Finally, it must have been
Much as you had imagined,

Having been cautioned, if not
By us, surely, in the end,

By what you'd come to expect,
How, the last cry and head-shake

Over, fat wives with blue hair,
Widows of used-car salesmen,

Would come to invade even
That solitude, unsummoned,

As you began to recede,
And settle, with no sound, far

Backward, into yourself, like
Some fountain turned off at dusk.

THE SURVIVOR

"Man feels himself lost, shipwrecked."

— Ortega y Gasset

Often he reappears now
In dreams, in a chill half-light,
Surfacing from the distance
As from a dark corridor,
Gesturing with his pale hands.

He stands on a deck, waiting.
As though in a photograph,
It is the same pose always.
The image is blurred, and he
Seems unaware of the cold,

Secretive life assembling
Outside the bottom edge of
The picture, submerged, hushed like
A reef expecting its ship,
His body preserved each time.

WEATHER REPORT
(To Wm Brown)

Brown, this is a short letter
about the wind, of a wind
you should remember, and how,

all morning, it has washed down
out of the arctic, over
the gold bulge of the prairies,

and how — I imagine it,
I'm sure, far too easily —
it must come from so removed

a place to arrive, as it does,
with such emotion (as though
distance were ever a guide),

and how — again, perhaps, I
overstate — I thought to see
it break like a wave upon

some shore in white hemispheres
unknown, yet, to me, tower
to the knife-edged passes, spill

downward across the tundra,
the bleached plains, the cold mosses,
working its way still deeper

into the mainland, combing,
always, from field to field, from
valley to valley floor, through

the heads of grain, the stiff corn,
the loose evergreen forests,
deeper and deeper until

it has come to lean against
this small house, rising upon
the windows, as if, somehow,

it wished inside and I must,
now, open the door, let it
enter . . .
        Brown, what is this wind?

No matter where you might be,
In what dream, on what cleared floor,
You would enjoy it down here.

As you are, asleep, the white
Covering you like a snow
(A snow risen to meet you
Completely), you are apart
From this; and yet it *is* you,
Or how we imagine you:

— The cactus, its chill spindles;
The green eye of the tiger . . .

And (now) behind these two, and
Taking its place among them:
The fire, the fire where you burn.

Outdoors, like a false morning,
Fog washes the pine trees. It
Shoulders against the windows,

Spreading across their surface
On its way upward. In this
Moment between sleep and thought,

This holding back, I can hear
The fog start to rise, the slow
Memory of an ocean,

And I, like a ship, begin
To stir, to lurch in its swell,
And to move outward, beyond

The steel jetty, the lighthouse,
The red-flagged channel buoys,
— Beyond, at last, sleep even —

Into a deeper water,
Pale, oracular, its waves
Motionless, seagulls absent.

Departures

Over Govino Bay, looking up from the water's edge, the landscape
   resembles nothing so much as the hills above Genova, valleying
   into the sea, washing down olive, cypress and excessive arbutus
   into the slow snapping of the plane trees where I, surrendering
   to the pulse beat of a silence so faint that it seems to come from
   another country, watch the sun rise over Albania, waiting —
   calmly, unquestioning — for Saint Spiridion of Holy Memory to
   arise, leave his silver casket and emerge, wearing the embroi-
   dered slippers, from his grove of miracles above the hill.

Corfu

It seemed, at the time, so indifferent an age that I recall nothing of
it except an infinite tedium to be endured. I envied no one, nor
dreamed of anything in particular as, unwillingly, I enveloped
myself in all of the various disguises of a decent childhood.
Nothing now comes to mind of ever embarking upon famous
voyages to the usual continents; of making, from the dark rooms
and empty houses of my imagination, brilliant escapes from
unnatural enemies; or, on rainy winter afternoons in an attic, of
inventing one plot or counterplot against a prince or a beast. . . .
Instead, it must have been otherwise.

I try to remember, nevertheless, something of all that time and place,
sitting alone here in a room in the middle of spring, hearing the
sound of a rain which has fallen for most of April, concerned
with such different things, things done by others. . . . I read of
the aimless coups in the old dynasties from Africa to Afghani-
stan, their new republics whose lists of war lords alone are
enough to distress the Aryan tongue; of intricate rockets in search
of a planet, soon, perhaps, to land in a country somewhere out-
side the pedestrian reach of reason; of the latest, old sailor's
account of a water dragon seen bathing off the grizzled coast of
Scotland. . . . It is at times such as this, and without thinking,
really, clothed in my goat's-wool robes, that I steal a camel from
an outlying Arabian stable, gather together my clansmen, and
gallop for days along the miraculous caravan trails to Asia.

At first I was overly cautious, procedure being all-important. I gathered around me those I considered friends, discovering, with a certain shock, a mere handful—nothing else, however, was lacking, as I had for months assembled equipage, and such rudiments as maps of cities, tidal charts, coastal readings, cryptic dictionaries, and guides to unusual monuments. Only, in assuring readiness, I had planned too well. . . . As it was, this much should have been warning.

For days on end we waited, close by the north-east docks, admiring the stubborn tugs at work, studying the sea lanes. Such depths of perfect skies over the gaudy ships, outward-bound through the gay whistles of sea birds! . . . And at night the glide and swish of well-oiled engines, the long calls of the horns. . . . The weeks lengthened, our patience thickening. Then something altered, if imperceptibly at first: perhaps some quirk of the weather, perhaps of the sea. A little later and it was unmistakable: things tended to incline together, fogging distinctions; ships became less common, and schedules grew erratic; destinations became unsure in my head; the nights were longer, and with them there was the uncontrollable desire for sleep, up till then only vaguely recalled. Eventually, even, some of my friends, sharers of the voyage, vanished. . . .

It is so difficult to come back, perspectives blunted, and to have only the waiting, now in the shuttered light, in the clutter of objects here in this drafty attic, until all is in readiness once more. Soon, perhaps, we shall go back down. But then, what stingy cargo to reload, what slackened baggage, O my stunted puppets!

The weeds have thickened among the orchards and leaves dangle
unnoticed under the archways. At nighttime, before, where
torchlight once peeled the darkness back from the lawn mosaics,
from the formal gardens, where, it has been rumored, the parties
attained such a perfection that Bacchus himself, angered at certain
tain contests staged in his name, peered in one twilight, then
ordered his image stricken from the household, his paeans dis-
continued, all is unshingled by the moon. Occasional chords
from a ghostly lute, it is true, will sometimes come down the
same Alpine wind that continues to herd the small waters into
the shore; or a strayed traveller, or some misguided pilgrim
might, of a summer evening, if he stands quite still and says
nothing, imagine he hears the slight off-rhythm of some hex-
ameter line deep in the olive grove, as the slither of night birds
moves toward the darker trees. But that is all.

Grotte di Catullo, Sirmione

STORM

And when, that night, the unseasonable rain (the hail a shredding
sound in the lemon trees) thudded against the lumbering of the
bay, in August, haunting the dark with a querulous whiteness,
he retired to the basement room under the house to study the
various aspects of water, the ships in sudden counterpoint on
the rising scales of the sea, and to wait for the breakthrough,
across the barren hills of his brain, of the bronze soldiers, for the
swelling flash of their knives.

Positano

Bolivar, Tennessee is where the state institution for the insane is located. These letters are to — not from — Bolivar. Number 8 is an adaptation from the French of Guillevic.

1.

At the foot of the stone wall
Where dogs, dappled and lank, nose
Through the damp spaces, the dark
Recesses where one might hide,
If, anymore, one were able to hide —

I think of you there, your face among all the others.
Death (someone will say) is easy
After the practice we have had:
The false starts, the perfect dress rehearsals.
I wonder . . .

2.

Siegfried Sassoon is dead.
The poet with the best name
Of the 20th century
Is dead — is dead, I said.

And all these years unheard of;
Remembered, only, because of friends,
A poet or two, who died in a war
(Some war) before all of ours.

Sunset. The sky, over Arkansas, inflames
Like the new flesh in a scar.

Did you read him? Do you care?
— Nobody ever does.

3.

Tonight, the blade of the new moon
Hangs upside-down above
The horizon, and gives no light.

Later, vanishing down the sky,
It enters beneath the curtains: I
— As the dark draws it deeper in —

Sit still, watching it move.

Must I, this time, lean out,
Give way to
Its thin comfort, its coppery edge?

4.

Wasn't it Eliot who said
The river is like a strong brown god?
I think it was. At least he
Said it most recently.
                    Here,
At the mouth of Wolf Creek, the river
Of Mark Twain, W. C. Handy and
The Mystery Tramp unrolls
Into the South (our South!) like a vein:

Where clouds are forming in monument
Over the Delta; where silence,
At dawn, spreads like a bruise; and where
— In the sun, in the rain —
The Man is at the crossroads, waiting . . .

              ❋   ❋   ❋   ❋

And love? Love is the cancer
Which makes us all
Play doctor O, play doctor.

5.

It is not, you understand, the bat,
That blind squeaker, I hear in the dark;
It is not, like a murmur of voices, the frog
Hidden within the oak — rather,
It is the owl, in his silent washings,
Floating across the moon,
Trailing his shadow like a change in the weather:
Over the fields, over the wall,
Over the low parts of the garden until
It enters, at last, the trees
Where it breaks into edges, edges that
Scatter along the leaves, resemble
The loose connections starting to drift, now,
Like cold seeds
                just under my skin.

6.

Consider de Maupassant:

He attained fame, then cut his own throat
At 40, in Cannes. Failing at this,
He was hustled back to Paris, to
A nursing home, where
He crawled about on his hands and knees
Eating his own filth.
The last line in their report read:
Monsieur de Maupassant va s'animaliser....
He died at 42,
                    his mother surviving him.

7.

Or Swift:

The premonition of madness (I
shall die like a tree — from the head
downward) confirmed, his
powers, according to Dr. Johnson, declined
until he lost distinction. Example:
within his room he would stare
at his plate for hours,
the meat thereon
— precut into small bites —
he would not eat while seated, but
as he paced, like a wounded thing, the floor.

After years of lying inert and silent
he died,
            expiring without a struggle,
what money he had being left
to found a lunatic asylum.

8.

There are those who must speak,
Speak on from the shadow in the corners
About wounds which knit with much pain
On the clearest of nights;

And of ponds which yawn
In the face of a wall
That would keep them down in their beds.

There are those who must hug
This wall, this same wall,

And try to open it
With words, with names yet to be found
For that which has no form
And has no name.

9.

I would say, off-hand, that things
Are beginning to happen:

The small, white chrysanthemum buds
Dangle like earrings from
Their pinched stems; the teeth
In my head, as though wired for sound,
Transmit a hot code;
The woman with red hair, whose neck
Is shaped like a forearm,
Closes her eyes, her black eyes,
And begins to sing.

Let's hear it out there; let's hear it!

(No one is listening)

10.

The leaves sink in the pool.
The leaves sink in the pool
Unpatterned, and cover the bottom.
They lie there, unmoving,
Without so much as a sigh.

On the pool's surface, insects
Are trundled about by the wind.

But wait! Like a clot of blood,
Working its way downward, a pome
From the pyracanthus drops toward the leaves.

Between the leaves and the insects,
Where the pome falls, the water
Is turning in on itself, over and over,
As though with a pure delight.

American Landscape

It lies in the American West
All but forgotten. No stone
Commemorates the spot,
Nor is one necessary. What hopes there
Have calcified, what expectations,
The traveller would not recognize;
Or — recognizing — care.

Such landmarks as showed the way
(The curious rocks, the morning clouds
Which were skulls) are scattered now,
Or have eroded. And paths

Which suffered our crossing, the roads which once
Existed, it seemed, merely
To take us there, have faded and overgrown.
Nothing is easily found. . . .

Should you persist, however, and should
You approach, tonight, that broken landscape you
Would find, at land's end, these words

'This is the grave of the right hand:
The threshold, the woebegone.'

PICCOLA ELEGIA
—*L. G.: Requiescat . . .*

Nicky, the word has come to the west coast
Of how you
Shuffled your feet, stammered,
And slipped out the back door

When no one was looking.
What did you have in mind?

         ❋   ❋   ❋   ❋

I picture myself back there,
In the kitchen, peering out
Through the glass, then through the orchard, your shirt

A small red dot among
The apple trees that run down
The long slope: the water
Glitters and flashes in

The cold sunlight; I try
To open the window, to tell you
To wait, to come back, but
It is too late, too
Late in the day; already

The boat is adrift; it is
On fire; the flames
Splash at the gunwales; and you
Are smoke, Nicky, you are smoke.

I have watched, I have listened for your answer
— The sound of a voice,
A footstep, a scratch at the window.

And this is no consolation, this light
Which oozes up from the sand
Wherever I walk, which marks a pathway,
And shows how I have arrived.

The fog is drifting in from Catalina;
The wind drops off; things vanish
And grow unlikely, or indeterminate:

Your future, like Shelley's glove, will lie
Encased in glass,
Predictable, disconnected:
The palm upturned, the fingers close together.

One of my father; he stands
In hunting clothes in front
Of our house; two dogs
Nuzzle the fingers of
His outstretched hand;
Under his right arm
The shotgun that now is mine
Gleams in the sunlight —
I cannot tell if he leaves
Or if he is just returned.

            ❋   ❋   ❋   ❋

One of my mother, and blurred;
Sunday; the afternoon
Is smoky and overcast;
Standing beside the lake,
She balances on a rock
At the waterline, gazing out;
Someone is in a boat
Taking her picture; she
Is waiting for them to land.
The water . . . The shoreline . . .

            ❋   ❋   ❋   ❋

This one of me at six
At play in the backyard —
Marbles of some sort;
The ring is quite visible
In the August dust;
I have Ups, and am fudging;
Off to one side,
A group of three boys:

One is my brother and one
Is someone I do not know.

    ❖   ❖   ❖   ❖

I shut the album hard.
What good are these now?
They do not answer *What next?*
Or *What was I trying to prove?*
They do not explain us:
Such poses are unrecorded —
They lurk like money, just
Out of reach, shining
And unredeemed:
And we hold such poses forever.

AFTERMATH

It is no longer mine, this stone,
Although it has been. It lies in my hand,
Now, as a stone will — cold, without regard.
What does it know of my hand that it stays so cold?

Recovered by chance, last night, in the new grass,
On it your message is written: in blood
— The blood of someone who does not know you yet —
And all but unreadable. But it is certain.

AMERICAN LANDSCAPE
—For Dick Runyan, in Montana

1.

It's April, still winter where
The otter and wolverine, the elk
And porcupine must search for food.

Down in the meadow, along the banks of the creek,
The ghost-weed and Indian paintbrush
Are several months away.

2.

There, in the Yaak, what will they say
As they ease you into your new life,
Indian, gyppo, child of the river's pulse?

What will they say in that small field
Heavy, now, with all of your family?

3.

We enter into the earth like shoots,
Throwing off tendrils, our fingers
Growing, joints loosening like water.

These roots go down forever,
Inch by inch, stone by stone, working
Toward some improbable center.

Above us, our single, unmoving branch
Gathers the sunlight and will not bloom.

4.

Up near Mount Caribou, the snow-owl

— Almost invisible against a white sky —
Planes down, looking for sleep;

The bear, feeling the new fingers take hold
In that hard earth, turns in his dream,
Thinking a flame has blown through his bones;

And the deer pause; and listen — hearing, it seems,
Your fingers dislodge the sharp stones.

    5.

What does one say? What *can* one say:
That death is without a metric,
That it has no metaphor?

That what will remain is what always remains:
The snow; the dark pines, their boughs
Heavy with moisture, and failing;

The clearings we might have crossed;
The footprints we do not leave?

Darkness dissembles; the lights recede
At random; bright
Pinpoints appear; valves hiss and unwind —

Isolate, far away, like breath
Escaping, the rush of blood
Dwindles to different chambers . . .

Meanwhile, the rinsings go on
And on, like an ocean,
Spilling into the flesh, rubbing

Their foamy edges into the grain.
Now there is no removal,

For these are the waters that burn,
The acids that scald;
These are the flames you have asked for.

The Lost Displays

— *While other people wore like clothes*
   The human beings in their days
   I set myself to bring to those
   Who thought I could the lost displays. . . .
                    — Philip Larkin

SELF-PORTRAIT

There is a street which runs
Slanting into a square
There is a marble hand

There is a pair of glasses
A statue also
Casting a long shadow

Someone is crossing the square
Nailed to a door
There is a pair of gloves

Over the crimson pods and dark styles
Of the oleander bush
The night bugs pivot and turn,
Yet do not land. How is it they know?

On the opposite wall, like the lines of some
Electroencephalogram,
The Virginia creeper spindles, trapping the light.

And nightshade, they say, is sure —
Two berries can kill a man.

     ❋   ❋   ❋   ❋

Already from the horizon, tossed
By the sea, the bottle
Has reached us — empty of anything, in pieces.

The pieces scatter and spell —
Like the styles of the oleander, and like the fruit,
They spell it out.

(And like, in childhood, those bits of glass
Taken into the flesh — which disappear,
Which leave no mark — will these, too, surface
In 25 years or so,
Uncolored, unedged, from our skin?)

Except the vermilion flesh
Around the seed, the yew
Is poisonous. The seed itself
Carries a giddiness, and attacks the heart.

(The bits of furniture, the old names
On the letter boxes, these stairs
Which I climb like an ill wind —
I feel like an image from
Some earlier poem
I am forced to rewrite and rewrite.)

Time will rescind? Certainly so —
Carve on a tree: whatever the name
It will crust in a season. Still,
It *is* a mark, your scar in my veins.

Polished and packaged, grotesque,
The fingers tapered
Like those a harpist might have —
What music would it play?

Probably none —
The intricate strictures in the glass
Would indicate otherwise.

An ordinary hand,
One without pain or distinction,
Except that it's here, except that it's waiting,
The object of no one's desire:

For look at the cut — there,
Below the palm, above the wrist:
A hand that offers itself, a hand to be kindled . . .

There is no hand for such hands, no pocket.

HALF-MOON

Consider the half-moon,
How it gains as it is failing;

How it finds its true fulfillment,
Yet remains to be fulfilled;

How it knows its own path,
And will rise through the night
With a cold eye
Having no fear, no pity —

Half-moons, might you rise

From the darkness of my fingertips
As you rise in the sky,

Without remorse, without excuse.

This, too, is an old story, yet
It is not death. Still,

The waters of darkness are in us.
In fact, they are rising,

Are rising toward our eyes.
And will wash against those windows

Until they have stilled, until,
Utterly calm, they have cleansed.

And then our lives will take substance,
And rise themselves.

And not like water and not like darkness, but
Like smoke, like prayer.

                                        Venice

Insensitive or discreet
In it the passions move

Seeking an entrance
In it the seasons meet

Mosslike with blood
Blended in clouds

The future a certain map
When the lid shuts

It is a reflection
It is a drawplate

The left and the right
Indistinguishable

Horses, black horses:
They carry the flames;
They cannot be shied.

The sparks from their hooves
Spread out through the night
Like stars, O like stars.

Wherever they pass,
The ashes drift down.
Wherever they pass.

Under the stone the lizard breathes,
His tongue a semaphore
In the blinking darkness;

Deep in the ribs of the oak's cage
The owl, like a new moon, appears;

Poised at the roof of the river's bed
The fish, thinking to rise, resists,
Fearing this gulp will be endless. . . .

❊   ❊   ❊   ❊

Neither the flickering from the stone,
Nor the owl's eye,
Nor the rainbow along the fish's side
Will show the way.

But there, where the fire ripens
(Where the fire is ripening like a spring),

The path will open, the Angel beckon,
And we will follow. For light is all.

0. Psittacosis
1. Cuckoopint
2. Reliquary
3. Pyxidium
4. Entelechy
5. Wyvern
6. White bryony
7. Zymotic
8. Contrapposto
9. Typolysis
10. Syzygy
11. Anti-matter
12. X
13. Carthago delenda est